Wheels and Axles

Andrea Rivera

abdopublishing.com

Published by Abdo Zoom™, PO Box 398166, Minneapolis, Minnesota 55439. Copyright © 2017 by
Abdo Consulting Group, Inc. International copyrights reserved in all countries. No part of this book may be
reproduced in any form without written permission from the publisher. Abdo Zoom™ is a trademark and logo
of Abdo Consulting Group, Inc.

Printed in the United States of America, North Mankato, Minnesota
102016
012017

THIS BOOK CONTAINS
RECYCLED MATERIALS

Cover Photo: Gabriel McEver/Shutterstock Images
Interior Photos: Gabriel McEver/Shutterstock Images, 1; Dave Long/iStockphoto, 4; iStockphoto, 5, 7, 9, 10–11, 14,
14–15, 17, 19, 21; Roni Meshulam Abramovitz/iStockphoto, 6; Darth Art/iStockphoto, 12; Shutterstock Images, 13;
Thongchai Pittayanon/Shutterstock Images, 16; R. D. Flemming/Shutterstock Images, 18–19

Editor: Brienna Rossiter
Series Designer: Madeline Berger
Art Direction: Dorothy Toth

Publisher's Cataloging-in-Publication Data
Names: Rivera, Andrea, author.
Title: Wheels and axles / by Andrea Rivera.
Description: Minneapolis, MN : Abdo Zoom, 2017. | Series: Simple machines |
    Includes bibliographical references and index.
Identifiers: LCCN 2016949163 | ISBN 9781680799576 (lib. bdg.) |
    ISBN 9781624025433 (ebook) | ISBN 9781624025990 (Read-to-me ebook)
Subjects: LCSH: Wheels--Juvenile literature. | Axles--Juvenile literature.
Classification: DDC 621.8/82--dc23
LC record available at http://lccn.loc.gov/2016949163

Table of Contents

A wheel and axle is
a **simple machine**.
It has two main parts.

The axle often looks like a rod. It has a wheel or wheels at its end.

The wheel
and axle turn
together.

They help people move loads.

Wheels and axles give a **mechanical advantage**. They make it easier for people to move heavy objects.

Wagons use wheels.
Pulling the handle supplies force.
Force turns the wheels.

It makes them roll.
This helps move
the wagon's load.

Engineering

Cars use wheels and axles.
A car has four wheels.

Two axles connect them.

The car's engine provides a force
that turns the axles.

The axles turn the wheels.
The wheels move the car.

Pottery wheels were invented thousands of years ago.

A potter puts clay on a wheel.
The wheel and axle turn.
This helps make clay bowls
and vases.

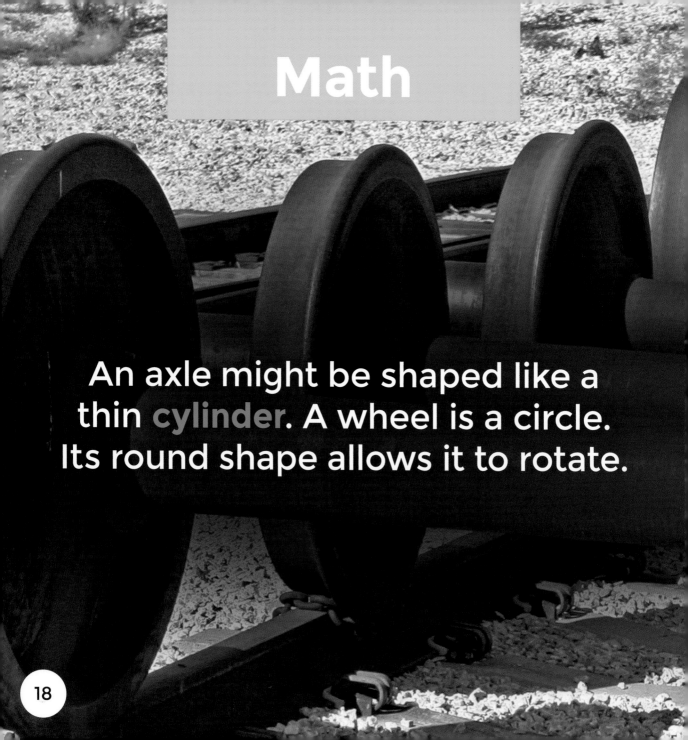

Math

An axle might be shaped like a thin cylinder. A wheel is a circle. Its round shape allows it to rotate.

The rolling wheel
makes work easier.

- Doorknobs, clock parts, and bicycle wheels are all examples of wheels and axles.

- In a doorknob, the axle goes through a hole in the door. The doorknob is the wheel. Turning it moves the axle. It opens the door.

- Ancient people used wheels and axles to help them move things.

Glossary

cylinder - a shape with flat, circular ends and sides shaped like the outside of a tube.

force - a push or pull that causes a change in motion.

load - an object that needs to be turned, lifted, or moved.

mechanical advantage - the way a simple machine makes work easier.

simple machine - a basic device that makes work easier.

Booklinks

For more information
on **wheels and axles**, please visit
booklinks.abdopublishing.com

Learn even more with the Abdo Zoom
STEAM database. Check out
abdozoom.com for more information.

Index